God
is
Three
in
One

By Jennifer Bosma

Illustrated by Beth Snider

God the Father

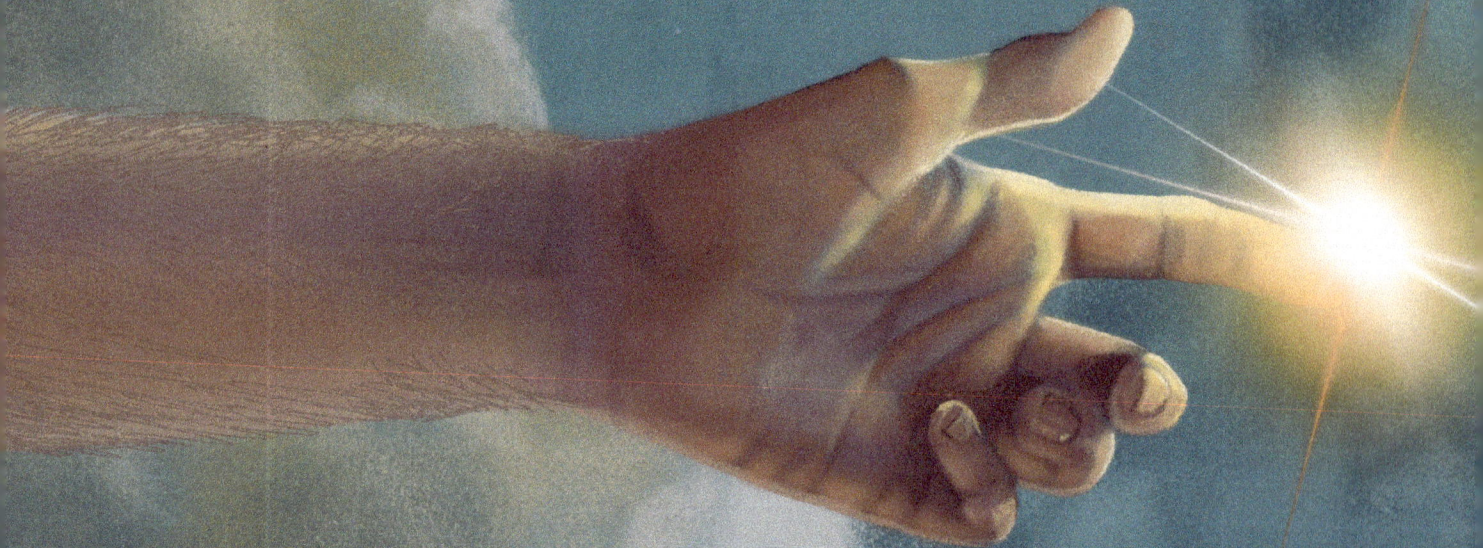

"In the beginning God created
the heavens and the earth."

Genesis 1:1 (NIV)

I see you, my child;
you're learning about Me.
I have plans for your life;
trust in Me to see.

I want you to know
that I am one in three,
So you'll understand
the Holy Trinity.

Let's start off at
the very beginning.
From the time that the
world started spinning.

I created the Earth,
and the birds that fly,
sunrise and sunset, and
the clouds way up high.

You'll see Me all around
if you are aware.
Talk to Me daily;
I have so much to share.

Adam and Eve were the
first people to breathe,
and they decided not
to listen to Me.

They did things the hard way;
sin came to the land
when they chose not to follow
My one command.

For years, people battled
and didn't hear My voice.
I spoke through the prophets,
but many made their choice.

Long before My Son would
come down as a man,
I shared with the world
He was always My plan.

When people were sinning,
and knew that they were wrong,
they'd look for an offering
and then move along.

Nothing they gave could
cover all of their sin.
To be free of guilt,
there was no way to win.

It was time for Jesus to
come to the Earth,
to save everyone by
the gift of new birth.

God *the* Son

"For God so loved the world that he gave his one and only Son, that whoever believes in him shall not perish but have eternal life."

John 3:16 (NIV)

I was born just like you,
growing up each day.
My parents and My Father
showed Me the way.

I knew I was different
because I am God's Son,
learning all His teachings,
and sharing how it's done.

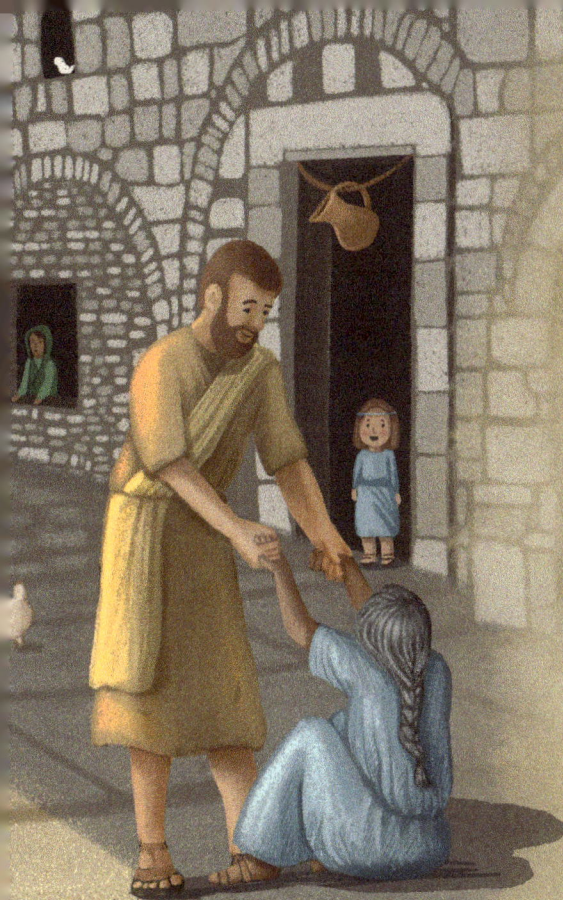

I chose twelve disciples
and shared from My heart.
I taught them God's way,
and they all played a part.

My miracles were seen by
the young and the old.
Many people believed,
but others just turned cold.

Some leaders were scared
and nailed Me to a cross.
I died, then I rose again;
all wasn't lost.

I paid the price for sins,
that someday will take place.
Follow Me, be forgiven with
My lasting grace.

I taught on Earth for forty days
and many did see,
I was alive, back from the tomb,
told in prophecy.

Then Heaven called and said,
"It is time for You to leave."
The Holy Spirit's here.
He will help you to believe.

God *the* Holy Spirit

"But you will receive power
when the Holy Spirit comes on you;
and you will be my witnesses in
Jerusalem, and in all Judea
and Samaria, and to the
ends of the earth."

Acts 1:8 (NIV)

Trust in Jesus,
I am with you today.
I'll give you power as
you learn to pray.

Follow God, not the world;
your path I will show.
And then you'll begin
to spiritually grow.

With Me in your life,
I'm three in one.
And My work in you
is far from done.

You're made in My image;
this was My plan.
I had you in mind since
the world began.

If you say this prayer and believe it's true,
Then eternal life has been given to you.

Dear Father in Heaven,
I need a new start.
Right now, I ask Jesus
to live in my heart.

Forgive me for all
the wrong things I do.
Help me to see things
from Your point of view.

I pray that my life may be
long and be blessed.
I promise to love You
and give You my best.

In Jesus' Name,
I pray, Amen.

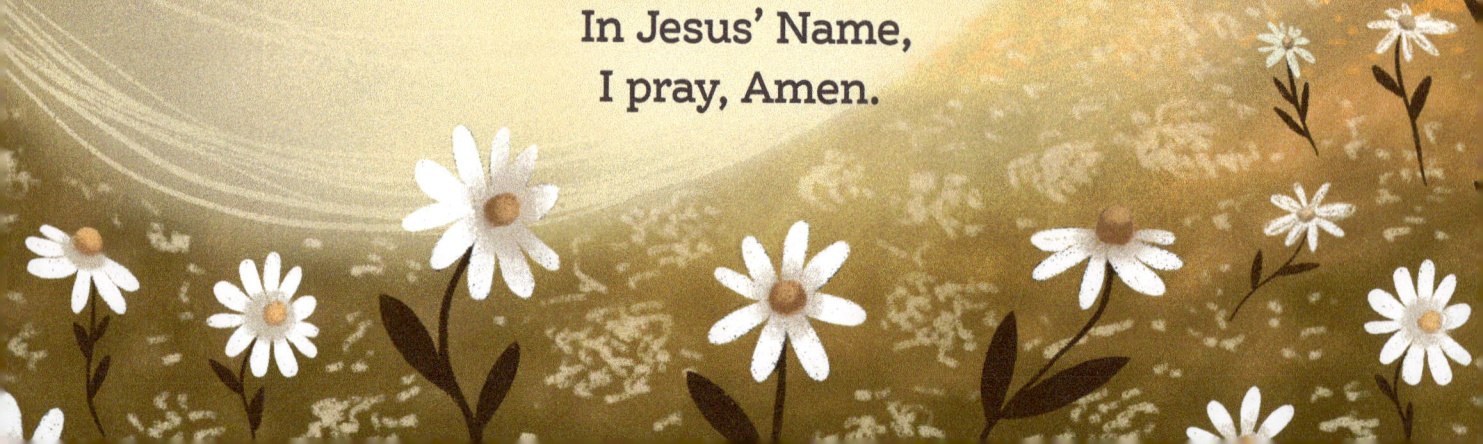

Yay!

For further study

Scriptures for the study of Jesus and the Holy Spirit in the New Testament

John 8:12 (NKJV)
"Then Jesus spoke to them again, saying, 'I am the light of the world.
He who follows Me shall not walk in darkness, but have the light of life.'"

John 14:6–7 (ESV)
"Jesus said to him, 'I am the way, and the truth, and the life.
No one comes to the Father except through me. If you had known me, you would have
known my Father also. From now on you do know him and have seen him.'"

John 14:16–17 (ESV)
"And I will ask the Father, and he will give you another Helper, to be with you forever,
even the Spirit of truth, whom the world cannot receive, because it neither sees him nor knows him.
You know him, for he dwells with you and will be in you."

John 14:26 (ESV)
"But the Helper, the Holy Spirit, whom the Father will send in my name, he will teach you
all things and bring to your remembrance all that I have said to you."

John 16:28 (ESV)
"I came from the Father and have come into the world,
and now I am leaving the world and going to the Father."

Luke 24:49 (NLT)
"And now I will send the Holy Spirit, just as my Father promised.
But stay here in the city until the Holy Spirit comes and fills you with power from heaven."

Some scripture prophecy of Jesus in the Old Testament

Isaiah 11:1-5 • Isaiah 53:1-12 • Psalm 22:1 • Psalm 31:5

www.ingramcontent.com/pod-product-compliance
Lightning Source LLC
Chambersburg PA
CBHW060944100426

42813CB00016B/2856